GOVERN LIKE A GIRL

KATE GRAHAM

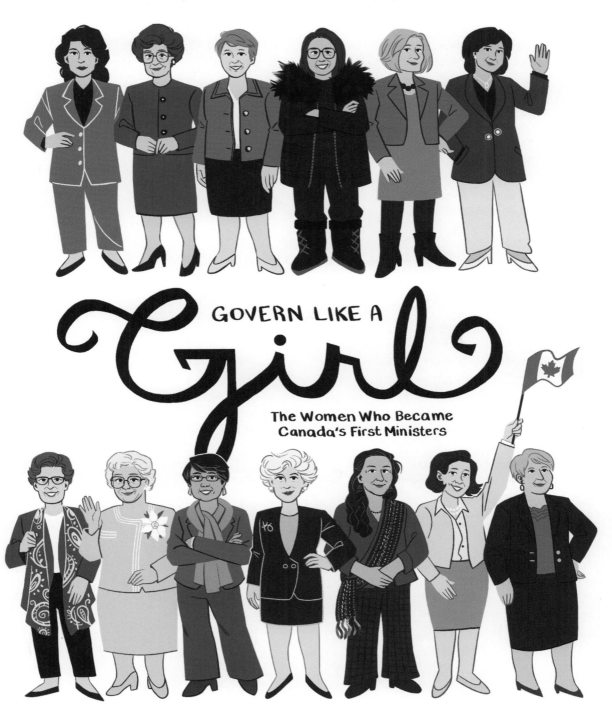

GOVERN LIKE A Girl

The Women Who Became
Canada's First Ministers

Second Story Press

Library and Archives Canada Cataloguing in Publication

Title: Govern like a girl : the women who became Canada's first ministers / Kate Graham.
Names: Graham, Kate, 1984- author.
Identifiers: Canadiana (print) 20210136146 | Canadiana (ebook) 20210136154 | ISBN 9781772602104 (softcover) | ISBN 9781772602135 (EPUB)
Subjects: LCSH: Women prime ministers—Canada—Biography—Juvenile literature. | LCSH: Premiers (Canada)—Biography—Juvenile literature. | LCSH: Women politicians—Canada—Biography—Juvenile literature. | LCGFT: Biographies.
Classification: LCC FC26.P6 G73 2021 | DDC j971.009/9—dc23

Edited by Andrea Knight

Illustrated by Liz Parkes

Printed and bound in Canada

Second Story Press gratefully acknowledges the support of the Ontario Arts Council and the Canada Council for the Arts for our publishing program. We acknowledge the financial support of the Government of Canada through the Canada Book Fund.

Published by
Second Story Press
20 Maud Street, Suite 401
Toronto, ON
M5V 2M5
www.secondstorypress.ca

For Flora
with love and hope

Premier
Pat Duncan

Premier
Caroline
Cochrane

Premier
Nellie
Cournoyea

Yukon

Nunavut

Premier Eva Aariak

Northwest
Territories

British
Columbia

Premier
Alison
Redford

Manitoba

Alberta

Saskat-
chewan

Premier Christy Clark

Premier
Rachel Notley

Premier
Rita Johnston

Premier Eva Aariak, Nunavut
Premier Catherine Callbeck, Prince Edward Island
Premier Christy Clark, British Columbia
Premier Caroline Cochrane, Northwest Territories
Premier Nellie Cournoyea, Northwest Territories
Premier Pat Duncan, Yukon
Premier Kathy Dunderdale, Newfoundland and Labrador
Premier Rita Johnston, British Columbia
Premier Pauline Marois, Québec
Premier Rachel Notley, Alberta
Premier Alison Redford, Alberta
Premier Kathleen Wynne, Ontario
Prime Minister Kim Campbell

Prime Minister
Kim Campbell

Newfoundland and Labrador

Premier Kathy
Dunderdale

Premier
Catherine
Callbeck

Québec

Premier
Kathleen
Wynne

Premier Pauline Marois

Ontario

Prince Edward Island

Nova Scotia

New Brunswick

Contents

Introduction

Who gets to make the rules in Canada? Who decides what we learn at school, or how many parks we have, or whether we take care of our environment?

The answer is the government—a group of people we choose to make decisions for us.

Once you turn eighteen, you can vote. You get to pick who you want to make the rules in your community, your province or territory, and your country. These people have the big job of doing what we call governing; making decisions that affect everyone.

Canada is a big country with lots of different people. We have young people and old people. We have people with black skin and brown skin and white skin. We have tall people and short people. We have people who use wheelchairs and people who need special help to hear or see or speak. We have people who like to be loud and people who like to be quiet. We have people who have different talents, like doing math or writing rules or taking care of others. We have people with many different kinds of experiences, like growing up in a big city or a small town or living in another country.

It's important that our governments are made up of all of these different kinds of people, with many different life experiences, so that when governments make decisions, those decisions help everyone.

But we have a big problem.

Most of the time, our governments don't have enough different kinds of people. Often, they do not include people from a diversity of backgrounds—and, they don't have very many women.

Women and girls are half of Canada's population but are only around thirty per cent of the people in our governments. And it's even fewer when we look at who gets the top job of being the prime minister or being the premier of a province or territory.

Canada has had twenty-three prime ministers, and only one was a woman.

More than 300 people have been the premier of their province or territory, and only twelve of those people have been women! Some provinces in Canada have never had a woman in charge.

This is a problem because it means that the decisions made by our governments might not always make life better for women and girls. It's one of the reasons that women and girls in Canada are more likely to be poor, more likely to experience violence, and often get paid less money at work. That is just not fair.

Questions for you:

- If you were in charge, what would you change about your community, your province or territory, and your country?

- What do you think happens when a big decision is being made and there are no girls or women there? Why is that a problem?

- What traits or skills do you think make someone a good leader? Do you have those traits and skills?

Who is the one woman who became the prime minister of Canada to lead our whole country? Who are the twelve women who have been the premier, in charge of their province or territory? What were they like when they were girls? How did they reach the top and what did they do when they got there?

In this book, you will meet the thirteen amazing women who rose to the top jobs in our governments. It wasn't easy—but they got there!

They showed Canada that women are great leaders and that it's okay for them to govern in their own way.

Canada has a long way to go before our governments include all the different kinds of people we have in our country.

This is where you come in.

No one else has the exact same opinions and knowledge and ideas and experiences that you have. No one. Only you know what matters most to you. If there is something you want to see change in our country, you need to tell the people in government who get to make those decisions. When you are old enough, you need to vote for the people you think will make the best decisions for you—or run for office yourself, so you can make the rules!

As the leaders in this book learned, you don't need to change who you are to be in charge. In fact, we need more people like you in government—people who know how to govern like a girl.

Visit **governlikeagirl.ca** to learn more

PREMIER
Eva Aariak

Eva Aariak has spent her life fighting for language rights for Inuit—and she knows firsthand why these rights are so important.

Eva Qamaniq Aariak was born in a camp on Baffin Island on a cold January day in 1955. Baffin Island is the largest island in Canada and the fifth largest in the world. It is a winter paradise located in the beautiful Arctic Ocean, home to whales, polar bears, walruses, and narwhals.

PREMIER
Eva Aariak

- Born in Arctic Bay, Northwest Territories (now Nunavut)

- Worked as a **news reporter** and **teacher** before running for office

- Appointed as the first **Languages Commissioner** for Nunavut

- Served as the second **premier of Nunavut** from 2008 to 2013

On the northern shore of Baffin Island sits a small Inuit community called Arctic Bay. Only about 800 people live in Arctic Bay today, but Inuit have lived in the community for more than 5,000 years. Inuit call Arctic Bay *Ikpiarjuk*, which means "the pocket," because the community sits at sea level surrounded by high hills.

When Eva was a young girl, she moved with her parents and older sister into her grandfather's house in Arctic Bay. The house had only one room.

Eva's parents had been self-sufficient for most of their lives, hunting and living off the land. Like many other Inuit parents, they decided to move to Arctic Bay when they had children so their kids could go to school.

Eva had a few older cousins who already lived in Arctic Bay. One day, when Eva was about five years old, she and her cousins were out playing near the school. Her cousins could see that Eva wanted to go to school, so they invited her inside. The teacher looked at Eva and began to speak to her in English, but Eva did not speak any English. The teacher sent her away, saying the one English word Eva did understand: *no*. She had to wait until she was older and could understand more English before coming back because lessons were taught only in English and not in Inuktitut, the language Eva spoke.

Living in Arctic Bay taught Eva what it meant to be part of a community. She could see how working together helped everyone. She also learned to be resourceful. Arctic Bay had only one store, the Hudson's Bay Company. Getting food or clothing was difficult, and homes did not have washing machines. There were few places for people to gather during the cold, dark winter months. So, on the weekends, the school would open up to the whole community. People would gather there at night to do their laundry together. The schoolteacher was also a photographer and taught weekend classes about how to take and develop pictures. And the clerk at the Hudson's Bay store was also an athlete who would lead exercise and gymnastics classes for the whole community.

Eva went to school in Arctic Bay for as long as she could, completing the highest level of school available in the small community. She wanted to continue to learn but doing so meant she had to leave. She moved hundreds of kilometres away from her family to Churchill, Manitoba to complete her studies before moving back to Arctic Bay.

Eva's first major political activity came shortly after her return home. Arctic Bay did not have as many recreational activities as she felt it should, but Eva had an idea. She wanted the local government to shovel the snow off a section of the frozen Arctic Bay so people could skate and play hockey. She requested an opportunity to speak as a delegate to the town council, asking for a Zamboni machine to be used to clear the ice. After her presentation, the council went into a closed room to discuss the idea. Eva was not allowed into the room. When they came out, they told her the answer was no. But, not long after the meeting, the ice was cleared off. The town's Zamboni driver had heard about Eva's presentation and cleared the ice anyway.

This sparked Eva's interest in politics. She learned that politics is about making decisions, and those decisions can solve problems and help people. She worked as a news reporter, telling the community about what was happening—and there was a lot! At the time, Arctic Bay was a part of the Northwest Territories. For many years, people wanted a large eastern area of the Northwest Territories to become its own territory. This idea had been discussed since before Eva was born. The Canadian government and Indigenous peoples had been in disputes over who owned the land for decades, and there were concerns that being a part of the Northwest Territories was threatening some parts of Inuit culture. The education system in the territory did not recognize Inuit languages spoken in places like Arctic Bay, so children had to attend school in English. After many years, agreements were finally reached, and in 1999 the new Canadian territory of Nunavut was created.

With the creation of the new territory, Eva was appointed to a new job as Languages Commissioner for Nunavut. One of her tasks was to choose a new word in the Inuktitut language for the Internet. Eva chose the word *ikiaqqijjut*, which means "travelling through layers."

Eva also became very involved in the community, volunteering with an Inuktitut-language book publishing program and chairing the Nunavut Film Development Corporation. She also opened a store in Nunavut's capital, Iqaluit, to sell Inuit arts and crafts.

People often told Eva that she should run for office to serve in the government. Eva had always been interested in politics. She watched debates and sometimes thought about what she would like to do if she were in a position to make decisions for her community and territory. By this time, Eva's children were adults and she felt a strong desire to do everything she could to make Nunavut a place where children could grow up with their own culture and language. She wanted to improve daycare services in Nunavut, for example, so more women could work and participate in civic and community life, including politics.

In 2008, Eva ran for the Nunavut Legislative Assembly— and she won! She was the only woman elected. Nunavut has a model of government called "consensus government." There are no political parties, and all the elected members make each decision together. After an election, all the elected members (called MLAs, or members of the legislative assembly) vote for which one of them will be the leader of the government: the premier. Eva put her name forward. She had big ideas about what she wanted the government to do in Nunavut. Three members wanted the job: the current premier, a male veteran politician, and newly elected Eva.

The vote was held on November 14, 2008, by secret ballot. After the ballots were counted, the results were announced: Eva Aariak had been elected as the first—and to date, only—female premier of Nunavut.

Even though she was the premier, Eva was also the only female MLA. Sometimes she found that her colleagues treated her differently or didn't listen to her. Sometimes she had to bluntly ask, "If I were a man, would you be treating me that way?" But Eva kept working hard to address the problems that people in Nunavut were experiencing. She worked to bring more mental health supports to the territory and introduced a better childcare system. She also worked to protect Inuit language rights. After serving as premier, Eva became the new Commissioner of Nunavut in 2021.

When she was a little girl, Eva never dreamt that she would become the premier someday.

"I never really imagined how far I would go. It was always about doing what I felt I could do, at that moment, in the community where I lived."

PREMIER
Catherine Callbeck

Catherine Callbeck knows what it's like to be the only woman in the room. She is also the only woman to date who has served as premier of Prince Edward Island (PEI). She was the first woman to become a premier in Canada by leading her party to an election victory.

Prince Edward Island, Canada's smallest province, is located in the Maritimes in the Gulf of Saint Lawrence. The entire province has a

PREMIER
Catherine Callbeck

- Born in Central Bedeque, Prince Edward Island
- Worked as a **teacher** and **business owner** before running for office
- Thought she was **too shy** for politics
- Served as the **premier of Prince Edward Island** from 1993 to 1996

population of about 160,000 people—about twenty times smaller than the population of the city of Toronto!

Near the southern coast of the island sits a small community called Central Bedeque. Today, along with its surroundings, it is home to about 300 people—including Catherine Callbeck, who still lives in the house where she grew up.

Catherine was born on July 25, 1939, into a well-known Prince Edward Island family. Her maternal grandfather and great-grandfather were both former mayors of Summerside. Her mother was a school trustee and her father ran a store called Callbecks, which became the largest country store in Prince Edward Island. Callbecks sold everything from clothing to building supplies to groceries, and also operated as the local post office and egg grading station. At its peak, Callbecks employed fifty people and generated sales of six million dollars per year—a large operation for the time and for Prince Edward Island!

Catherine attended a two-room school near her home and was involved in the family business from a young age. At twelve, she stocked shelves, served ice cream, and helped customers. Watching her father run the business, she also learned how to manage money. One summer, in addition to working at the store, she helped to harvest a three-acre plot of strawberries. Instead of spending her wages, she put all the money she was paid into her savings account.

Catherine was a strong student. When she graduated from high school, she was accepted to Mount Allison University. She wanted to study business, but this was not a normal choice for a woman at the time. Catherine enrolled anyway. She was the only woman in the Bachelor of Commerce degree program in 1956 and the second woman to graduate from Mount Allison with this degree.

After graduation, Catherine decided she wanted to teach business. She applied for a job at a high school in New Brunswick and was offered the job with a salary of $3,500 per year. This was $500 less than the male teachers were paid. Catherine refused the offer, telling them that it was because of the unfair pay. She later accepted the job when it was offered to her at $4,000 per year.

After a few years of teaching business, Catherine decided that she wanted to get back into the business world herself. Her father had passed away, and her brother Bill was running the family business. Catherine returned home to Central Bedeque and she and Bill began expanding the Callbeck store with a new furniture department.

For many years, people had told Catherine that she should run for political office. At first, she felt she was too shy. This changed in 1973, when Prince Edward Island was celebrating its centennial (100th) year as a province. Catherine was asked to chair a centennial committee for eight communities, and they organized a highly successful event. That was Catherine's invitation into public life. In 1974, she decided to run as a Liberal candidate in the Prince Edward Island provincial election. At that point, only one woman had ever been elected to the provincial legislature. Not everyone supported Catherine's decision to run. One man Catherine knew well said to her, "I know you have been successful at many things, but I can't support you because you're a woman."

Catherine persisted. In her speech to secure her party's nomination, she said, "the strength of a society rests on the willingness and ability of its citizens to share in the decisions which affect it." She recruited many young people, including young women, to help her on the campaign. It paid off, and she won. Her party also won the most seats, forming a majority government.

Shortly after the election, the premier announced his new Cabinet. Catherine was named minister of health and social services, two large and demanding portfolios. Once again, Catherine was the only woman appointed to Cabinet. She became the first woman and youngest person in Prince Edward Island to hold a Cabinet portfolio.

After four years in the provincial legislature, Catherine decided to step away from politics and went back to work in her family business

for a decade. Then, on her 49th birthday, Callbeck announced a return to politics—this time at the federal level. She ran and won her seat as a member of parliament (MP), where she served for more than four years, and then made another major step. When the premier of Prince Edward Island announced his resignation in 1992, a leadership campaign was launched. Catherine received many calls asking her to consider running. At first she said no, but after careful re-evaluation, she felt this was an opportunity to do more for her province. Once again, she ran and won, becoming the first—and to date, only—female premier of Prince Edward Island.

One of the hot political issues was the idea to construct a fixed link—a bridge or tunnel—between Prince Edward Island and mainland Canada. This idea was not new. There had been proposals about a fixed link since the 1870s, when the Canadian railway system was expanded. Over the years, many options had been considered. In 1988, the question of whether or not a fixed link should be built was put to plebiscite, a direct question put to all eligible voters, which allowed PEI residents to vote on the matter. A group called Friends of the Island organized opposition to the idea, claiming the project would damage the environment and harm the Prince Edward Island lifestyle. Another group called Islanders for a Better Tomorrow organized support for the fixed link because of the economic benefits it would bring to the island. In the end, Islanders voted almost sixty per cent in favour of building a link.

However, the project was not without its challenges. The costs were high, and the initial studies to construct a bridge were challenged in court by Friends of the Island. The project required a constitutional amendment to free the federal government from its obligation to provide a steamship service between PEI and the mainland. Callbeck was concerned that when the bridge was completed, the ferry service would be discontinued. She obtained firm assurance from constitutional experts that this amendment would not affect ferry service and she agreed to proceed. Leaders at other levels of government had changed, and the project was losing political support.

Catherine, as the new premier, pushed forward and pushed hard. Once again, it paid off. Construction of the Confederation Bridge began in 1993, and the bridge opened in 1997. It is Canada's longest bridge, and the longest bridge over ice-covered water in the world.

After her time as premier, Catherine went on to serve in the Senate of Canada and as the Chancellor of the University of Prince Edward Island. She has been the first woman in many roles during her life and continues to be a champion for women in leadership, politics, and business.

PREMIER
Christy Clark

Christy Clark learned from an early age that politics isn't just about winning.

Christy was born on October 29, 1965, in Burnaby, British Columbia (BC). Her mom, Mavis, was a family therapist. Her dad, Jim, was a teacher. Christy was the baby of the family, joining two older brothers and an older sister.

Christy Clark

- Born in Burnaby, British Columbia
- **Longest serving** female first minister in Canadian history
- Hosted her own **radio show, The Christy Clark Show**
- Served as the **premier of British Columbia** from 2011 to 2017

Some families don't talk about politics. That wasn't the case for Christy. Her family often sat at the dinner table together and talked about the headlines and issues of the day. Her dad was particularly engaged in politics and ran as a candidate in three elections while Christy was a kid. Jim was a candidate for the British Columbia Liberal Party, but the party had little public support at the time, so winning was unlikely. Still, he put his heart and soul into each campaign. Christy and her siblings helped out, folding brochures and going door-to-door with their dad. On election night, her family had a party to celebrate the end of the race, even though Jim never won. He had contributed to the debate and raised important issues in each campaign—that itself was cause for celebration.

Christy went to university and joined a campus political club as a way to make new friends. The campus club organized university students for the BC Liberals, the same political party Christy's dad had run for when she was a kid. There was an election on the horizon, and being considered a serious candidate meant that the leader of the party needed to be included in the television debates. He needed to have candidates running for his party in every riding in British Columbia. Christy and a friend she met in the campus club (and later ended up marrying) made it their mission to find enough candidates. They travelled around British Columbia asking people to run for office.

The party (like almost all political parties) did not have enough female candidates. Christy quickly learned how difficult it can be to recruit women to run for office. Women often carry greater family responsibilities, caring for children and aging parents, which can make it difficult to run. In other cases, women may have a harder time imagining themselves as political leaders—in part because there have been so few women in political leadership roles in Canada. Christy continued to ask people to run, and the party ended up recruiting enough candidates for the leader to be included in official debates.

Christy also found that she had the political bug! She moved to Ottawa and got involved in federal politics, working on the national youth campaign for the future prime minister, Jean Chrétien, and then working for a federal cabinet minister. She enjoyed working as a staff member and never imagined running herself.

And then, opportunity knocked. Christy's brother Bruce was at the airport when he ran into Gordon Campbell. Gordon was a former mayor of Vancouver and had just become the new leader of the BC Liberal Party. Bruce said to Gordon, "You know, you should get my sister to run for you." Not long after, Christy got a call from Gordon, asking her to run. She thought about it and then agreed. She moved back to British Columbia and started her first campaign. In 1996, Christy ran for the same party her dad had run for years before—and she won.

Christy's political career started in opposition (the party with the second most seats forms the official opposition to the government), since her party did not hold enough seats to form government. This changed after the 2001 election. Christy was re-elected and this time her party won enough seats to govern. She was appointed minister of education and deputy premier—a rapid rise for such a newly elected official. She also gave birth to a son while serving in Cabinet, making her only the second woman in Canada to do so (after Pauline Marois).

Being a mother and being in politics was challenging. In 2004, Christy announced that she was leaving political life to spend more time with her son. She became a well-known media personality, hosting *The Christy Clark Show* on the radio, writing weekly newspaper columns, and appearing on television as a political commentator. It seemed that her own political career was behind her—until opportunity knocked once again.

Premier Gordon Campbell announced his retirement, sparking a leadership race to choose the new leader, who would also become the premier. Even after five years away from provincial politics, Christy decided to run. Her platform included establishing a Family Day holiday in February for all of British Columbia. She did not have much support from the elected members of her party, but she ran a strong campaign. In February 2011, Christy won the leadership contest, making her the leader and the new premier of British Columbia.

Her first major test came in 2013 as the province went into another provincial election. It was the first general election with Christy as premier and leader. The polls predicted that she and her party would lose the election badly. By this point, the party had been in power for almost a decade and had made decisions that were unpopular with some British Columbia residents. But Christy surprised some of the political experts by leading her party to victory.

This was not the only major election surprise while Christy was premier. The next one came in 2017. There are 87 seats in the legislative assembly of British Columbia, so a party needs to win 44 seats to form a majority government. Christy led her party to win 43 seats. The other two largest parties, which won 41 seats and 3 seats, decided to join together and form a coalition. Through a vote of non-confidence, the coalition was able to defeat the Liberal government. The coalition parties became the new government, and Christy resigned.

Christy Clark is the longest serving female first minister in Canadian history. She was premier for six years. She led the party her dad had run for through two election campaigns, both with more favourable results than were expected. Now, she has returned to her roots by asking women to run for office. She knows firsthand how difficult it can be to recruit women but also knows the impact that women can have by stepping up to run.

"My view of life is that opportunities are raining down around us all the time. Some people have fewer opportunities, as their circumstances haven't put them in a particularly rainy spot—but, opportunities are always there. Look around, figure out what opportunities are there, and choose which ones to grab."

PREMIER
Caroline Cochrane

In September 2019, the Council of the Federation—the assembly of the premiers of every province and territory in Canada—was entirely made up of men. That changed in October 2019 with the election of Caroline Cochrane as premier of the Northwest Territories.

Caroline's father was a diamond driller. He worked in Ontario and then moved to northern Alberta in the 1950s in search of

PREMIER
Caroline Cochrane

- Born in Flin Flon, Manitoba
- Was the **CEO** of the Centre for Northern Families before running for office
- Leads a non-partisan **consensus government**
- Elected as the **premier of the Northwest Territories** in 2019

gold. He met a Métis woman, fell in love, and started what became a large family of eight children.

When Caroline was two years old, her family moved north to Yellowknife, in the Northwest Territories. Caroline enjoyed life in the North, including close-knit communities, wide-open spaces, and the spectacular Aurora Borealis sky on clear evenings. But her family began to experience major challenges. At age 13, Caroline left home and started living on her own. With limited education and work options in her younger years, she struggled between having no housing and living in unsafe/unstable housing. She learned the hard way about struggles that people face and was later motivated to help them.

The birth of her second child and the separation from their father brought the realization that she had to change her life. She returned to school, obtained a degree in social work, and started her career working to support low-income families and women who were experiencing homelessness. She worked in this field for two decades and became the chief executive officer of a major social service organization.

Caroline was successful, but she was frustrated. She worked with people facing serious struggles and felt that the people in power didn't care. She knew firsthand about the lack of supports available in the North, as well as the much higher cost of living. She saw people from southern Canada coming to the North, making major decisions, and then leaving. She also believed there were great opportunities for northern communities that were not being pursued.

Caroline often complained to her husband about these problems. One day, he got upset with her and said, "Caroline, you need to put your money where your mouth is, then. You need to run for politics."

Caroline laughed at the idea, but a few days later she saw an ad in the newspaper about a workshop for women considering running for office. The program was run by the Native Women's Association and the government of the Northwest Territories' status of women office. Caroline and her friend Julie Green, a reporter and business owner in Yellowknife, attended the workshop. It covered the basics of running a political campaign: the election rules, how to recruit volunteers, how to raise money, and more. The workshop was in 2014 and the next general election was in 2015. After the workshop, both Caroline and Julie decided to run.

Caroline quickly realized that she didn't know much about politics. One day, she was out knocking on doors, and a woman answered the door. She told Caroline that her husband would like to meet her, and she went inside to get him. A few moments later, he joined Caroline on the front step.

"Do you know who I am?" he asked.

"No, but I think I've seen your wife somewhere."

He didn't identify himself, but they spoke for a few minutes about the election ahead. As Caroline was leaving, he reached out to shake her hand.

"Thanks for running. My name is Joe Handley."

When Caroline got home, she looked him up on the Internet only to find out that he was the former premier of the Northwest Territories. Ironically, he became one of her greatest supporters.

Caroline worked hard on her campaign right up until the election in November 2015. When the results came in, only two women had been elected to the legislative assembly: Caroline Cochrane and Julie Green.

There are no political parties in the Northwest Territories. People run as independent candidates in their ridings and the winners form the legislative assembly for the territory. The members of legislative assembly (MLAs) then vote amongst themselves who will be premier and hold the various minister portfolios. The premier, Bob McLeod, had been in the role for eight years. In 2019, he announced that he was not seeking re-election as premier. Four MLAs—two women, including Caroline, and two men—decided to run to be the new leader and premier. After three rounds of secret ballots, Caroline won. Julie Green became the minister of health and social services, and responsible for seniors and persons with disabilities.

One of the first things that Caroline wanted to do was meet with other women premiers. Unfortunately, as her staff told her, "There are no other women right now. There's only you."

Caroline knows the barriers that women face, both from her own life experiences and from her professional work. She also knows how important it is for women to be at the table to make decisions that help people.

"I'm a social worker at heart. I'm used to listening and really hearing people. I know that women have to work twice as hard to get half the recognition, so darned if I'm not going to do that to make sure I can be a role model for other women. So, I keep going."

PREMIER
Nellie Cournoyea

Nellie Cournoyea is probably the only human on Earth who has received five honourary doctorates, been named to the Aboriginal Business Hall of Fame, and made a member of the Order of the Northwest Territories and an Officer of the Order of Canada. And it all started because she spotted problems that she wanted to solve.

Nellie Cournoyea

- Born in Aklavik, Northwest Territories
- Worked as a **radio announcer** and **station manager** before running for office
- First Indigenous woman and second woman in Canada to become a first minister
- Served as the sixth **premier of the Northwest Territories** from 1991 to 1995

Nellie was born in 1940 in a small hamlet called Aklavik in the far northwest corner of the Northwest Territories, near the Alaska border and the Arctic Sea. Her father was a trapper from Norway and her mother was an Inupiaq woman from Yukon. She grew up on a trapline, hunting along the Western Arctic coast. As a child, she was sent to a residential school, as her mother had been as well. At one point, she ran away from the school.

Aklavik had always been a tight-knit community. There was no running water or electricity, so people had to work together to haul water, cut wood, hunt, and live off the land. Life was very busy. As the oldest girl in the family, Nellie was also expected to help her mother with cooking and raising her younger siblings.

In the late 1950s, life in Aklavik came under threat. The oil and gas industry had moved quickly into the region. The riverbanks were being washed

away and major flooding occurred on a regular basis. The federal government's solution was to build a new community, Inuvik, with the intention of closing Aklavik. There were tense discussions about land ownership and resources.

At the time, Nellie was working at the CBC radio station as an announcer and station manager. The community was angry about the federal government's decision. They had lived self-sufficiently for generations, and suddenly they were being forced to leave and change everything about their lives. People agreed that someone needed to speak up and fight back.

Nellie co-founded the Committee for Original People's Entitlement (COPE) to speak on behalf of the people in her community. Nellie and COPE became actively involved in negotiations with the federal government to settle land claims for the region. It was a frustrating process, and many people felt that the government didn't really understand the realities of life in the area or what was at stake. People started to encourage Nellie to run for office so she would be in a position to make decisions within government. She agreed, and in 1979 she was elected to the territorial legislative assembly.

Once in government, Nellie took on many leadership roles, including as minister of health, of social services, and of energy, mines, and resources. She also continued to work on the land claims negotiation. Some people made a joke about the fact that she never wore dresses or "dressed like a girl." In response, Nellie promised that once the land claim was settled, she would wear a dress. In 1984, after more than a decade of negotiations, Nellie showed up after the final agreement was reached—wearing a dress.

"I assure you, this is not my dress," Nellie said. "I've always told them that you can't boss people around unless you are in pants and a little bit sweaty. I am doing this tonight, just for all the people who worked so hard, and I'll give it back to [her friend] Frieda when I'm finished with it."

In 1991, after twelve years as an MLA, Nellie's colleagues elected her to serve as premier of the Northwest Territories. She was the second woman in Canada (after Rita Johnston) to serve as premier, and the first Indigenous woman to do so.

Nellie's remarkable accomplishments and contributions are widely recognized, including honourary doctorate degrees and major awards. But for Nellie, it has never been about the recognition.

"Living in a survival society, you learn a lot. You're very conscious of what is going on around you—and the participation of everyone becomes very important. I wouldn't say I was ever interested in politics, as politics is known. We were expected to take part in the community. It was not a desire to be a politician or based on a plan. It was an evolutionary need to do something about something. So that made it very real."

PREMIER
Pat Duncan

The morning after Pat Duncan was elected as premier of Yukon, the *Globe and Mail* newspaper assumed that she was a man and reported that "Mr. Duncan" had won the election. It was not the first time Pat surprised people by doing what few women had done before.

Pat's parents met while serving in the military. Her father, from Scotland, was a Royal Air Force pilot and her mother, from the United States,

PREMIER
Pat Duncan

- Born in Edmonton, Alberta
- Worked as a **small business owner** before entering politics
- Served as the **premier of Yukon** from 2000 to 2002
- Now serves as a member of the **Senate of Canada**

served in the Canadian Armed Forces. They met in Ottawa. They fell in love, married, and moved to the United Kingdom, where they had four babies while living at various air force stations in Great Britain. In 1955, the couple decided to immigrate to Canada with their children and found their way to Edmonton, Alberta. Shortly after they arrived, a fifth and final baby joined the family: Pat.

Pat's parents encouraged all their children to dream big. Her father was a strong feminist, meaning that he believed that men and women should have equal rights and opportunities. He believed that women could do anything they put their minds to and would often say, "They can because they think they can, Patricia Jane. Do you think you can do it? Then do it."

This became Pat's attitude, too. She got involved in many activities in her community and her participation often led to leadership roles. She joined the Girl Guides and rose to be the provincial commissioner. She joined the curling team, and represented Yukon at the Canada Winter Games.

Pat learned that she had a particular skill as a communicator. When she spoke up, people listened—and she wasn't afraid to use her voice. Many of her curling teammates were very shy. Competing at a major national sporting event meant that sometimes the team was asked to speak. "Pat," her teammates would say, "you go and speak on our behalf." She became the communications representative on her school council and sometimes spoke in front of her whole school or on the radio.

Pat graduated from Carleton University in Ottawa and then returned to Yukon. She ran a small business and was hired as the executive director of the Whitehorse Chamber of Commerce. This job gave her many opportunities to speak up on behalf of people and businesses in her community.

People sometimes told Pat that she should run for office. She was asked to run for mayor of Whitehorse, to lead the city council, and to run for various political parties at the provincial and federal level. Pat loved politics but turned down all these offers. Her career was going well. She also didn't feel that politics was a place where women were welcome. After all, there were few women in politics. This feeling changed in 1995, when a man named Ken Taylor, leader of the Yukon Liberal Party, asked Pat to meet him for lunch.

"You don't have money for lunch," Pat told him. "You need to save money for an election. Let me make you lunch."

Over a homemade lunch, Ken shared with Pat his vision for Yukon, which included seeing more women in leadership roles. He asked Pat to run for his party in the next election.

At the time, Pat had a one-year-old daughter and she and her husband were considering having a second baby. That night, Pat talked to her husband about Ken's request for her to run in the next election. "What happens if I run and I get pregnant again?"

Pat's husband wasn't fazed at the idea. "Well, we would figure it out."

She agreed to run in the election. And shortly after, she found out she was pregnant.

Pat got to work. She knocked on doors in her riding to introduce herself to voters and ask for their support in the upcoming election. She gave birth to a son, and the election was called shortly after. Taking care of a new baby and running in an election was very tiring. Pat's opponent told voters that Pat "just had a baby" to discourage them from voting for her, suggesting that as a new mother she wouldn't be able to do a good job as an elected official. One day, about a week before the election, Pat knocked on the door of yet another voter who had heard this message.

"I don't know if I can vote for you. Didn't you just have a baby?"

Pat was frustrated. "If I was a man coming to your door, would you ask me that question? Tony Penikett (a former Yukon premier) and his wife had twins while he was running for office."

The woman stepped back. "Oh my. I am so sorry. I'm a lifelong feminist. I'm really sorry I asked you that question. And yes, I'll vote for you."

Pat's hard work paid off. On election day, she was elected to the Yukon Legislative Assembly. However, her party did not do well. Ken did not win his seat and resigned as leader of the Yukon Liberal Party. Pat was one of just three members of the party to be elected—the other two were father and daughter. So Pat, as a newly elected MLA and new mother, became the party leader.

Rebuilding a political party after an election defeat is hard work. Once again, Pat's ability to communicate became an important ingredient in recruiting new candidates and members and convincing the public that the party was ready to govern again. In 2000, Pat led her small party through an election and this time, they won. The Yukon Liberals won the majority of seats and formed the new government. Pat became Yukon's first female premier.

As premier, Pat worked to make life better for everyone in Yukon. She was particularly interested in addressing laws that disadvantaged some people over others. She kept a reminder in her office of a law that was included in the *Canada Elections Act* in 1890:

"No woman, idiot, lunatic or criminal shall vote."

She knew that law, which prevented women from voting, didn't change until a group of women fought to change it. And having women in places where laws are made is an important step toward passing laws that treat women fairly and equally.

Pat sometimes worried that being elected to office shortly after the birth of her son meant that she was not able to spend as much time with him as she should. After all, very few women with young children run for office in Canada—let alone lead a party. After being premier, Pat went on to work in government and then later was appointed to the Senate of Canada. She has now dedicated most of her working life to public service.

One night at dinner, she asked her children whether they suffered as a result of her running for office.

Her son looked surprised. "Mom, what are you talking about? That's just what you do."

Pat's friends who were also mothers put it this way: "You taught your children what women can do and what women are capable of. You led by example."

PREMIER
Kathy Dunderdale

As a girl, Kathy Dunderdale never imagined that she would become premier of the province she grew up in, but when her community was facing a threat, she stepped up to help and one thing led to another.

Kathy's parents, Norman and Alice Warren, lived in the town of Burin, a small fishing community located along the southern coast of Newfoundland. The Burin Peninsula is often called the "boot" of

PREMIER
Kathy Dunderdale

- Born in Burin, Newfoundland and Labrador
- Worked as a **social worker** before running for office
- Started her political career in local government, serving as **deputy mayor** on the Burin town council
- Served as the **premier of Newfoundland and Labrador** from 2010 to 2014

Newfoundland because of how it is shaped, and the town of Burin is located in the "heel."

Norman and Alice had eleven children, including Kathy. Their house was a rambunctious and noisy place, with a large dinner table frequently hosting conversations about the politics of Burin, Newfoundland, and Canada. Newfoundland joined Canada in 1949, making it the tenth province to enter Confederation—and this was hotly debated at the time. Alice in particular loved to debate about politics and always encouraged her kids that if they had something to say, they should say it. Kathy and her siblings grew up with an understanding that politics mattered because it had such a big impact on people's lives. Paying attention and being engaged was important.

Like most families in the small community, Kathy's family relied on the fishing industry. Her dad, Norman, was a fisherman. Sometimes he would go out, catch lots of fish, and bring home a paycheque that would support his large family. Other times, he would come back empty-handed. In the small community, people learned to rely on each other and help each other out through hard times. Sometimes, that meant her family had to accept help from other people, and sometimes it meant there were a few extra kids at the table at her house come dinnertime.

In the 1980s, the multinational corporation that owned the Burin fishery decided to shut it down. By this time, Kathy had grown up and was married to a master mariner who spent a lot of time out at sea, while Kathy stayed home looking after their young children. Kathy knew what the decision to shut down the fishery would mean for so many families in her community, and she knew she needed to do something about it.

Kathy started a citizen action committee to fight back against the closure. She gathered a group of people, and they barricaded the plant and ships. They stood hand in hand and refused to move unless someone from the company would negotiate with them. This got so much attention that the company agreed to at least talk to Kathy and her group and sent some of their senior executives to little Burin. The citizen action committee got ready, doing research and preparing their arguments. Over the course of a year, they went back and forth with the executives. Finally, a decision was made: the fishery would change some operations but would stay open, and the people who worked there could keep their jobs.

This event started Kathy on a political journey that she had never imagined. She was elected to the Burin town council and then became the deputy mayor of her community. She got involved in a national organization called the Federation of Canadian Municipalities that included thousands of cities and towns across Canada. She even became the first female president of the organization. Kathy got involved in advocating for her town and local governments across Newfoundland and Labrador to the provincial government.

Kathy was no stranger to sexism. Many of the roles she took on were not places where many women had served. She could feel that she was sometimes not treated with the same respect given to her male colleagues. She had also experienced sexism in her personal life. Once, while her husband was out at sea, Kathy and her young children went to visit the construction site of the house they were building. Kathy was pregnant and they needed more space for their growing family. The man at the site asked, "Where's the man who's building this house?" Kathy replied, "This will be my house. I'm here." The man didn't want to speak with her about the project and continued to ask, "But where is the man?"

Kathy was undeterred by these experiences. If anything, they pushed her to keep showing that women can do what men can do.

In 1993, Kathy left her council seat to run in the provincial election because she was angry about the way the provincial government was treating local governments. She ran against a well-established cabinet minister in a riding she didn't live in. She knew she wouldn't win, but she did it anyway to send a message and be part of the debates. She lost but became a respected part of the provincial Progressive Conservative Party.

She decided to run again—and this time, she won. The premier, Danny Williams, saw Kathy's leadership potential. He appointed Kathy as minister, responsible for several major portfolios, and then as deputy premier. When the premier decided to step down, Kathy was appointed the new premier of Newfoundland and Labrador. She was the first, and to date only, woman to  hold that position. As premier, she worked to make government more efficient, and spoke up about provinces and territories needing to work together on important issues.

Kathy has a favourite book that she reads once a year about the important role that women—including her grandmothers—played in the founding of Newfoundland and Labrador.

"They would be astounded that their granddaughter became the premier; to imagine that someone who was a part of them might one day lead the place they helped build. We have come a long way."

PREMIER
Rita Johnston

Rita Johnston made history when she was the first woman in Canada to become premier, but she never lost her values or forgot her humble roots.

Rita was born on April 22, 1935. When she was six years old, she moved to Vancouver, British Columbia (BC) with her parents, John and Annie Leichert. Rita was never interested in some of the things her

Rita Johnston

- Born in Melville, Saskatchewan
- Operated a **trailer park** in Surrey, British Columbia before entering politics
- Served as the **premier of British Columbia** in 1991
- Was the **first woman** (ever!) to be a premier in Canada

friends were interested in, like playing with dolls. She did get excited when her mom bought her a stationery set. She liked reading and writing and teaching Sunday School at her local church.

Six days after Rita turned sixteen, she married George Johnston, her high-school sweetheart. She worked in the office of a finance company, and George worked as a forestry millwright. Rita and George had three children. When the kids were teenagers, the couple pursued their dream of opening a new trailer park in Surrey, BC. Little did Rita know at the time, building the trailer park would end up leading her along a very different path.

While she and George were developing the park, Rita often had to use services at city hall. This sparked her new interest in politics. She saw firsthand how important the decisions being made by people in government were for her, her family, and her business. When the next municipal election came along, Rita ran for Surrey city council—and won.

It was the beginning of what would be a remarkable political career. In Surrey's 1969 election, Rita was elected as a new alderman (yes, her title was "alderman" even though she was a woman!), and a man named Bill Vander Zalm was elected as mayor. The two became strong political allies and worked together on many projects. Bill left council for provincial politics and was elected as a member of the legislative assembly (MLA) in British Columbia. After a few years, Bill decided to step down to run for mayor of Vancouver. This created an opening for a new MLA—so once again Rita ran, and won.

It was an interesting time to be a new MLA in British Columbia. Not long after the election, the premier and leader of Rita's party, the Social Credit Party, announced that he was retiring. A leadership race was called. Rita thought that Bill should be the leader. She encouraged him to run and, when he agreed, she worked on his campaign. By the time the leadership convention came around to choose a new leader, there were twelve candidates in the race. After four rounds of voting, Rita's work on Bill's campaign paid off: he was elected as leader and became the premier of British Columbia.

Rita was appointed to lead several important ministries, including looking after transportation and highways, and the province's relationships with local governments. In 1990, Bill appointed Rita to be the deputy premier of the province—a decision that ended up making Canadian history. Not two years later, Bill resigned from office. Rita became the leader of the Social Credit Party and the first woman in Canada to be a premier.

The day after Rita became premier, a newspaper story asked, "What to call a 'lady premier'—Mrs? Ms? Madame?" They had never had to address or write about a woman in the role before.

Rita served as premier for six months. She took on the leadership at a time when the party was unpopular and heading into an election. Her party lost the election, as she did—but, she will forever go down in the record book for breaking a very important "glass ceiling" for women.

Rita never lost sight of how politics matters to people's everyday lives.

"I have down-to-earth values, you know. Bread-and-butter concerns."

PREMIER
Pauline Marois

Pauline Marois' story is one of resilience, an example of the times when you have to try and try and try again to get where you want to go.

Her story begins with a young couple, Marie-Paule and Grégoire Marois, who were married in the 1940s in Quebec City, the capital of Québec. Québec is the second largest province in Canada and the one province in Canada where French is the only official language. Quebec

- Born in Quebec City, Québec
- Worked as a **social worker** before running for office
- First woman in Canada to **have a baby** while serving as a cabinet minister
- Served as the **premier of Québec** from 2012 to 2014

City is a special place, one of the oldest cities in North America. The "old city" is a UNESCO (United Nations Educational, Scientific and Cultural Organization) World Heritage Site. Grégoire was a heavy-machinery mechanic and built a small brick house for his growing family. Marie-Paule and Grégoire had five children together. The oldest was named Pauline.

Pauline was raised to believe in the importance of education. Her father regretted not having been able to continue his studies and wanted his kids to get university degrees (which they all eventually did). Pauline loved studying French, history, and geography. She won awards at school and received a scholarship to attend a private school. It was a shock to her system. She was raised in a working-class neighbourhood and had never met people from such wealthy families. Even as she studied with her affluent classmates, she sometimes helped her mother clean houses to pay the bills and take care of her younger siblings.

This experience gave Pauline a deep appreciation for the inequalities in her province. Children from poorer families lived in inadequate housing, faced a lack of services, and often received a lower-quality education. At the time, the Quiet Revolution—*la Révolution tranquille*—was taking place in Québec. This was a period of rapid social change that included changes to the province's education system. Pauline became more and more interested in the political revolution taking place, especially in protecting French-language rights and addressing inequalities faced by the Québécois (people who were born in or lived in Québec).

Pauline studied at the Université Laval and then began her career in social work. She became the chief executive officer of a *centre local de services communautaires*, a free health clinic run by the provincial government. After she completed a master's of business administration (MBA) degree at the Université de Montréal, she decided to get involved in politics.

It was a contentious political time. In 1980, Québec held a referendum —a vote by citizens—about whether Québec should move toward separating from Canada. Sixty per cent of people voted against the idea, but Pauline supported it. She was approached to run for office by the leader of the Parti Québécois, the political party leading this movement. At first, she was hesitant. She had a good job and she and her husband were about to have a baby, but she decided that the issues of the day were too important for her to sit on the sidelines. Pauline

ran in the 1981 Québec election, and won. At the age of thirty-two, she was named minister for the status of women in Québec. Eleven days later, she gave birth to baby Félix.

Pauline quickly became an important and influential figure in Québec politics—but that didn't stop her from taking risks. When the premier announced his resignation in 1985, she ran for leader. She came in second. She was also defeated that same year in a general election. Undeterred, she became involved in the leadership of the Fédération des femmes du Québec, which focused on promoting women's rights in Québec. She ran for office again in 1988 and lost. But she didn't give up.

In 1989, Pauline was once again elected as a member of the national assembly (MNA). She was re-elected in 1994, and this time the Parti Québécois also won the most seats and formed government. She was sometimes described as the "minister of everything" because she took on so many important roles. As minister of education, one of her most important accomplishments was to introduce a $5-a-day subsidized childcare program for families across Québec.

In 2005, Pauline's party had another leadership race. Once again, Pauline placed second. The person who won only lasted for two years and led the party through one of its worst election defeats. He resigned, and another leadership race was held. Pauline ran for leader for the third time. The party was in such poor shape that no one else ran. Pauline was named as party leader with a big task ahead of her: to rebuild the party and try to win back support from the people of Québec. It would be a long road with many challenges along the way.

The most significant moment of Pauline's career arrived on the night of the 2012 Québec general election—thirty-two years after Pauline first entered politics! She led her party to an election victory and formed a minority government, becoming the 30th premier of Québec and the first (and to date, only) woman to lead the province.

It was an important and historic moment in Québec, but that evening also had a tragic side. As Pauline was delivering her victory speech, a man entered the hall with a semi-automatic rifle, intending to shoot Pauline. A technician who tried to stop him was shot and killed. Pauline's security crew escorted her offstage as the police immediately apprehended the man. Moments later, Pauline returned to the stage to calm down the crowd and asked people to leave. She later attended the funeral of the technician who was killed, the person who perhaps saved her life.

Pauline's political career, which spanned almost thirty-five years, had many twists and turns. She would not have broken the glass ceiling in Québec if she had given up along the way.

As Pauline said after one election defeat, "For me, everything is still possible. The project of a people does not die."

PREMIER
Rachel Notley

Politics has been a part of Rachel Notley's life from day one.

In 1963, a twenty-four-year-old man named Grant Notley ran for office for the first time. He had just graduated from university a few years before and had a passion for politics. He came in last in the election—but it marked the beginning of a two-decade-long political career during which he became the leader of his party, the Alberta New Democratic

Party (NDP). That election also marked the beginning of another new adventure. Ten months after the election, Grant and his wife, Sandra, welcomed a baby girl named Rachel into the world.

When Rachel was seven years old, she moved with her parents and two brothers to the small Alberta town of Fairview. Her father was elected as a member of the legislative assembly, representing a large rural district in northwestern Alberta. Being an elected official and leader of a political party meant that he was away a lot and could only come home a few times each month. When he was home, Rachel and her brothers would watch their dad run around responding to constituency issues. Sometimes it was a farmer calling because the department of transportation had knocked down a fence and their cattle were escaping. Other times, it was someone calling about an issue with education or health care.

For Rachel, watching her dad taught her a lot about politics. Grant's party held only one seat in the legislative assembly—his seat! There was another political party that was very powerful, and Rachel saw her dad stand up to this party about the things he believed in. Rachel's mom, Sandy, described her dad's job to young Rachel as being "like Robin Hood"—he was trying to get money from the people who had a lot to help the people who needed it. Sandy was also very engaged in politics and took Rachel and her brothers to antiwar protests when they were kids.

When Rachel was twenty years old and studying at Grande Prairie Regional College, she received a horrible phone call. There had been a plane crash overnight and six of the ten people onboard had been killed, including Rachel's father. Elaine Noskiye, an Indigenous woman with fourteen children and who had just given birth, was also killed that night. She had been away to receive medical care and was finally returning home to her family. It was a very sad time in Alberta and for Rachel's family.

Rachel finished her undergraduate degree and moved to Toronto to attend law school. She was surrounded by students who wanted to get high-paying jobs on Bay Street, the Toronto street where many of the largest law firms in Canada are located. She realized that wasn't her path. After graduation, she dreamt of returning home to Alberta and using her law degree to help people living in poverty—the same people her father cared so much about.

Along the way, Rachel took on many new challenges. She worked for a large union, representing workers who were injured on the job.

She moved to Vancouver to work for the attorney general of British Columbia and helped to expand laws that would protect same-sex couples. She also got involved in an organization that advocated for the rights of kids with special needs. Rachel loved the law, but she also found it frustrating. She felt that she was arguing the same cases over and over again to fix problems created by the laws that were in place. Eventually, she realized that she wanted to change the laws. It was time for her to run for office.

In 2006, Rachel was nominated as a candidate for the Alberta NDP, the party her father had led many years before. There was so much excitement about Rachel running for office that one of her heroes, Jack Layton, flew in to attend her nomination. He was the leader of the federal NDP. Two years later, when the election came around, Rachel was elected as a member of the legislative assembly (MLA). She was re-elected in 2012 with a higher percentage of votes than any other MLA.

In 2014, the leader of the party announced that he was resigning, and many people asked Rachel to run for leader. It was a hard decision. She had young children and she could remember from watching her dad just how demanding a job it would be. She decided to have a conversation with her husband and kids about it. As a family, they agreed that Rachel should run for leader—and so she did. And in October 2014, she became leader of the Alberta NDP. The next day was the 30th anniversary of her father's death.

What the family didn't know was what that decision would mean. Like her dad, Rachel was leading a party that had never formed government. The leader of the party had never become premier of Alberta. The province was heading into an election, but the party in government had won every election for forty-four years.

Rachel and her team campaigned hard. Heading into the election, they held four seats in the legislative assembly. The polls started to show that the Alberta NDP might do better than they expected. Rachel started to think that they might win fifteen seats, which would be a historic victory for the party.

On election night, the results were even better. Rachel's party won fifty-four seats and formed a majority government for the first time. Rachel became the second woman to be premier of Alberta, after Alison Redford. She had led her party to a level of success that would have made her father very proud.

As premier, Rachel continued to be motivated to help people in Alberta, just as she had before she got into politics. She created the province's first ministry of women's affairs and ensured that half of the Cabinet were women—including two pregnant women. She introduced a gender-based analysis of government policy, which meant that they had to consider how girls and women would be affected by every decision they made. She raised the minimum wage to the highest level in the country at the time, and phased out coal power plants to clean the air and fight climate change.

In Rachel's words, "If you believe in something and you think it's going to make a real difference in the lives of people, you have to work for it—and if you're up against the odds, well, just work even harder."

PREMIER
Alison Redford

Alison Redford has seen more of the world than most people ever will—and she's tried to help people in every place she's been.

Her story begins in Glasgow, Scotland, with the union of two hard-working people. Her grandfather worked in the mines in Scotland, a difficult and sometimes dangerous job. Her granny was the oldest of thirteen kids and was sent to work at a candy factory from the age of

PREMIER
Alison Redford

- Worked as a **lawyer** before running for office
- Has lived and worked in countries **all over the world**
- Served as the **premier of Alberta** from 2011 to 2014

fourteen, to make money for her family. The two met, married, and had four kids, including Alison's mother, Helen. The couple decided to immigrate to Edmonton, Alberta, and it turned out to be a good decision. Alison's grandfather quickly found work and used any extra money he earned to help other newcomer families. He helped them find and fix up houses so they would have a place to live, just as he and his family had done. He earned a reputation for being someone who helped other people.

Alison's mother, Helen, inherited her parents' openness to moving around the world. She married an electrician named Merrill, and they decided that they wanted to see the world. They moved several times as a young family. By the time Alison was twelve years old, she had lived on both coasts of Canada (in British Columbia and in Nova Scotia), in Alberta, and in Borneo, a large island in southeast Asia.

Living in so many different places meant that Alison saw people who lived very different lives. She saw people who lived in poverty. She saw people who didn't have basic things that most families in Canada enjoy. And, importantly, she saw that often these inequalities were simply the result of the situation or place that someone was born into. For Alison, it also sparked what would end up being a lifelong ambition to help people all over the world.

Alison's family was very hardworking, but no one had ever attended university. Alison was a bright child and did very well at school. After graduating high school, she went to the University of Saskatchewan and completed a law degree. She quickly got to work using her legal training in countries around the world.

She was sent to do human rights work in Africa, Asia, and the Middle East. She helped create new laws that would remove barriers for girls attending school. She helped fight for people who faced violence and oppression.

One of her most important assignments was in Afghanistan. Alison was appointed by the Secretary-General of the United Nations to administer the country's first parliamentary election. A big part of Alison's job was helping women vote, many for the very first time. Once, Alison was headed to meet with a group of women in one of the most dangerous parts of the country. She was held up by security and arrived more than three hours late. She was worried that everyone would have gone home by the time she got there—but when she arrived, there were more than sixty women and their daughters packed into a school classroom. They had risked their lives to be there, and they had waited for more than three hours to learn from Alison how they could vote.

For Alison, every new job meant moving to a new place—but she also began to grow more and more worried about what was happening at home in Alberta. She saw political decisions being made that were hurting people. She felt some of the leaders were doing things that would help them get elected but were creating division and inequality—exactly the kinds of things her grandfather would have stood against as a new resident of Alberta. So, she made a big decision: it was time to move home and run for office.

Her first attempt was not successful. She tried to challenge a sitting elected official—a man—and the Progressive Conservative (PC) Party didn't want her to run. She experienced some of the ways that Canadian democracy can be rigged to benefit some people over others. Being home, she also became more upset about the direction her province was going—and was even more motivated to change it.

In March 2008, Alison was elected as a PC member of the legislative assembly (MLA) of Alberta. Despite being a brand-new MLA, she was also named attorney general for the province. She served on many different committees including the treasury board, which makes important decisions about how the government should spend money.

These new roles involved a major change in Alison's life. She and her husband had a young daughter and made the decision that they would try to limit the impact of Alison's political life on their daughter. They decided that Alison would travel but the family would not move. They bought a house right across the street from their daughter's school.

Not three years into her first term, the leader of the party and premier of Alberta announced his resignation. People immediately began asking Alison to run. They told her she could win. Alison didn't want to run because she knew what that would mean for her family. But, she also knew that she wanted to make major changes in both her own party and her province. She felt important issues like strengthening democracy, mental health services, and LGBTQ rights were not getting the attention they deserved. And so, after much consideration, she decided to run. It turned out that the people who said she would win were right. In October 2011, Alison was elected leader of her party and became the first female premier of Alberta.

Alison's daughter was raised watching her mom do something that no woman had done before, and she saw the challenges that come with blazing a new trail. Surely these experiences will influence Alison's daughter, just as watching her parents and grandparents shaped Alison's outlook on life.

"I've always thought about politics and government as being trying to make society better. There are circumstances that have made some people in the world vulnerable, and we have an obligation to help. It's just a matter of treating other people the way you would want to be treated—with respect."

PREMIER
Kathleen Wynne

Kathleen Wynne believes in the power of education—a passion that she discovered as a very young girl.

Her story begins with John Wynne and Patsy O'Day, a young couple who married in the early 1950s. John was a family doctor who grew up in the Toronto area, and Patsy was a musician who was raised in the Bahamas. The couple decided to raise their family in Richmond

PREMIER
Kathleen Wynne

- Born in Toronto, Ontario
- Studied and worked in **education** before running for office
- Served as the **premier of Ontario** from 2013 to 2018
- Was the first openly **gay premier** in Canada

Hill, Ontario. Their first child was a girl named Kathleen, born in 1953. Two more baby girls followed shortly after, and later one more, completing the family of four daughters.

As the oldest child, Kathleen was the first among her sisters to go to school. She absolutely loved it. She would come home from kindergarten at the end of the day and play school with her sisters (even when they didn't really want to). Kathleen always played the teacher and her sisters always played the students.

Kathleen's parents were both interested in politics and encouraged debate around the dinner table. Kathleen learned early that there were problems in the world and that politics was a way to solve them. Kathleen's grandmother, who was a teacher until she got married, wanted her granddaughters to know how important elections were. As a woman born in the 1880s, she wasn't allowed to vote until she was more than thirty years old. She didn't take her right to vote for granted and didn't want her granddaughters to, either.

Although Kathleen loved school, it was also a place where she first encountered inequality—systems and rules that helped some people and hurt others. Growing up in a family of girls, it was the first time she experienced boys and girls being treated differently. In kindergarten, this included things like boys playing with the blocks while the girls were expected to play with dolls. Kathleen didn't think it was fair that she couldn't play with blocks just because she was a girl.

As she grew older, she began to fight back against these inequalities. She wasn't afraid to speak up about rules she thought needed to be changed. One example was when Kathleen started high school, the school rules required the girls to wear skirts to school and the boys to wear pants. Kathleen and her friends organized a protest where one day all the girls would wear pants to school. She was sent home by the principal for breaking the rules. Kathleen's mother Patsy—who herself had often challenged rules she thought needed to change—happily wrote her daughter a note saying that Kathleen should be 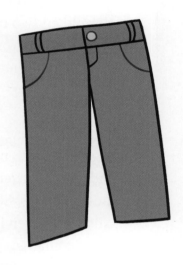 allowed to return to school wearing whatever she wished. Other girls' mothers did the same. And the school changed the rule: girls could wear pants if they wanted to, just like the boys.

In Kathleen's last year of high school, she decided to run for student council. She wanted to run for president, but there were a number of young men who were already running. She stepped aside and ran for secretary instead. She was acclaimed—no one ran against her—but it was a motivating experience for her. She reflected on why she had allowed herself to be discouraged from running for president. She vowed that she would fight against the barriers—especially in education—that prevented women from enjoying equality with men. And, she did.

Kathleen graduated from Queen's University and then completed two master's degrees, one in linguistics and one in education. When she had children, she became involved in their school councils and then ran as a school trustee.

In 1995, a new premier was elected in Ontario and began making major changes in areas like education and local government. Kathleen strongly opposed these changes. She believed they would make the education that some kids were receiving much worse. She also didn't support the province's forcing changes on local governments, particularly when citizens opposed them. Kathleen started a group with a few other women who also opposed the provincial government. The group met each week at Kathleen's house and talked about what they were going to do. Their numbers started to grow so much that soon they didn't fit around Kathleen's table anymore! So many people joined their movement that they had to meet in community centres and churches. At the peak, more than two thousand people came out to their meetings. This group eventually became known as the Metro Parent Network.

As these movements gathered steam, Kathleen became even more motivated to make change. In 2000, she was elected as a school trustee. During her campaign, she experienced yet another injustice—homophobia, prejudice against gay people. Flyers were distributed saying hateful things about her because she was a lesbian. She didn't give in and once she was elected, she helped pass new rules to address homophobia by teaching kids that families can include two parents of the same gender.

Kathleen didn't stop there. In 2003, she was elected as a Liberal member of provincial parliament (MPP) in Ontario, defeating someone who had been part of the government she opposed so strongly. She worked hard to represent her constituents and make changes she wanted to see in Ontario.

One of the things Kathleen wanted to change was a rule that if a student dropped out of school, they would not be allowed to get a driver's license. She thought this was a very bad idea. For students who dropped out for health or family reasons, for example, this could create a major barrier in their lives. She asked to meet with Ontario Premier Dalton McGuinty about the rule. When they sat down for the meeting, Kathleen was ready to present her argument, but Premier McGuinty surprised her with a question instead: "Will you be the minister of education for Ontario?" he asked.

Kathleen was shocked—and delighted! She agreed and they talked about this new role. Kathleen got up to leave, and then remembered why she had set up the meeting. "Premier, can I fix the driver's license thing?"

Premier McGuinty laughed. "Oh, for heaven's sake," he said. "Yes."

In 2012, Premier McGuinty made another surprising announcement: he was retiring from politics. It was time for the Ontario Liberal Party to choose a new leader. Many people asked Kathleen to run. Others told her that she shouldn't run and that Ontario voters wouldn't elect a lesbian premier. There had never been an openly gay or lesbian premier anywhere in Canada.

Kathleen decided to run. There were seven people in the race and some people didn't think Kathleen was going to win. During her speech in front of thousands of people at the old Maple Leaf Gardens (and hundreds of thousands more watching on TV), she directly addressed the concern that people had about her running as a lesbian woman. "I don't believe the people of Ontario judge their leaders on the basis of race, colour, or sexual orientation. I don't believe they hold that prejudice in their hearts."

When the votes were counted, it turned out that the members of her party agreed. Kathleen was elected as the leader of the Liberal Party and the new premier of Ontario.

Kathleen's grandmother had been a teacher but was forced to quit her job when she got married. That was the rule in the 1920s. Kathleen grew up knowing that when something is unfair, people need to stand up and change it. Thinking about the barriers that women like her grandmother faced gave her the motivation to do it.

"I remember my grandmother talking about how she had to stop teaching. She loved her teaching years—so there was always some sadness around women's opportunities that I grew up with, and I think that fueled my sense of indignation."

Kathleen's willingness to stand up for what she believed in and push for changes she wanted to see led her all the way to the top job in Canada's most populous province. No other woman has reached this peak—at least, not yet.

PRIME MINISTER
Kim Campbell

Only one woman has ever risen to the most senior political role in Canada—prime minister—and she'd spent her whole life reaching for the top.

But let's start at the beginning.

PRIME MINISTER
Kim Campbell

- Born in Port Alberni, British Columbia
- Worked as a **lawyer** before running for office
- Was a **co-host of CBC's Junior Television Club** as a kid
- The only woman to date to serve as **prime minister of Canada**

George Campbell and Lissa Cook met during World War II when George was stationed at Port Alberni, British Columbia (BC). The young couple fell in love and married in 1944, just months before George was sent overseas. Four months later, he returned to Lissa and a new three-month-old daughter, Alix. Shortly after, the couple welcomed a second girl: Avril Phaedra Douglas Campbell.

While Alix and Avril were growing up in Vancouver, their parents were drifting apart. They sent the girls away to a boarding school in Victoria. Young Avril considered it a great adventure and excelled at the school. One of her teachers claims she was the only student during her entire career to get every question right on an IQ test.

When Avril was twelve years old, she and her sister received some bad news: their mother had left and moved to Europe. Avril and her sister wanted to go home to be with their father, but he felt it was best for them to finish the school year. Avril announced shortly after that she had decided to change her name from the one given to her by her mother. From this point forward, she was known as Kim Campbell.

Kim had a steadfast ambition to succeed. She became the top student at her school. She was a disciplined musician and a published poet, elected the first female student council president, and was class valedictorian. Kim completed an undergraduate degree in political science at the University of British Columbia—but  she still didn't know what she wanted to do. She studied for a master's degree and a PhD, and then taught courses at university. After a few years, she decided to take a different path and went to law school. From there, she entered politics. Kim ran for the Vancouver school board and won. Shortly after, at the age of thirty-six, she became the school board chair.

Serving on the school board excited Kim's interest in British Columbia's provincial politics. She ran as a Social Credit member of the legislative assembly (MLA), but lost. She then took a bold step and ran to lead the BC Social Credit Party. Once again, she lost—placing last—but her speech at the convention caught many people by surprise. She spoke passionately about the kind of changes she wanted to see in BC politics and some people considered it to be the best speech of the race. She ran a third time to become an MLA—and this time, she won. This victory began her rapid rise in Canadian politics. She served as a provincial MLA for three years and then decided to run for federal politics. In 1988, Kim was elected as a Progressive Conservative member of parliament (MP).

Almost immediately, Kim was given senior leadership roles. Shortly after the election, she received a phone call from the prime minister, Brian Mulroney. He asked if she could meet with him at 7:00. She immediately booked plane tickets for her and her husband to travel from Vancouver to Ottawa for the meeting. She arrived, tired from the flight, and she and her husband went out for dinner. While they were eating, she got another phone call. It was the prime minister. When he asked, "Where are you!?" Kim was horrified. He had wanted to meet with her at 7:00 p.m., rather than 7:00 a.m. the next morning as she had assumed! The prime minister of Canada was waiting to meet with her, and Kim hadn't shown up! "We should be having this conversation in person," he said, "but I'd like to name you as a minister in my cabinet."

This was a major step. As a minister of state for what was then called Indian Affairs and Northern Development, she would have the opportunity to lead the country's work on building relationships with First Nations. After serving in this role, she was asked to take on another leadership role, becoming the minister of justice and attorney general, responsible for Canada's justice system. She was the first woman to hold both of these roles. As attorney general, Kim led major changes, including putting restrictions on the use of guns and providing more support for women who experienced sexual assault. She also introduced major legislation that expanded women's rights in Canada.

In February 1993, the prime minister announced that he was retiring from politics. A leadership race was called to choose the new leader for the Progressive Conservative Party. Because the party was in government, the new leader would automatically become prime minister. It was a difficult time to become a new leader as an election was just months away and the party was doing poorly in the polls.

Many people asked Kim to run. The party needed a dynamic new leader, and Kim was well respected for her work in Cabinet. She was also known as a powerful speaker. But the country had never had a female prime minister. Would people vote for a party led by a woman? Some people worried that having a female leader might hurt the party in the election.

Kim was up for the challenge and decided to run. There were four men in the race. Kim travelled across the country to speak to party members—the people who would be voting for the new leader. By the time she got to the leadership convention, she had built a large team of supporters. She walked onstage to the song "A New Sensation." She made a  speech about why she wanted to lead the party and Canada—and she won. Kim Campbell became the 19th prime minister of Canada on June 25, 1993. She was the first woman to rise to Canada's most senior political office.

There was no time to rest after winning the leadership race. The party was heading into a general election and, as a new leader, Kim had to convince Canadians that she was up to the job of continuing to be their prime minister. She again travelled across the country campaigning, while also doing the work of prime minister. She quickly introduced major changes to the structure of Cabinet to make it work more efficiently.

During the election campaign, there were many challenges. Kim's party had been in power for a decade and many Canadians were not happy with a number of decisions the government had made. Kim's campaign also released a commercial with nasty video footage of her opponent, Jean Chrétien. Kim did not see the commercial before it was released, but the public responded very negatively to an advertisement making fun of Chrétien for having partial paralysis in his face.

On election night, the results were clear: Kim and her party lost. Of the 295 seats in the House of Commons at that time, Kim's party only won two seats. After 132 days as prime minister, Kim's political career came to a close. She was later appointed by Jean Chrétien as consul general, a diplomatic representative of Canada, in Los Angeles. She chaired the Council of Women World Leaders, a global organization of women who have served as their country's president or prime minister. She continues to hold a variety of leadership roles.

Kim's talents, skills, and ambition led her to a political peak that no other woman in Canadian history has yet to reach. She learned that she could use her voice to make change happen.

In Kim's words, "When I was in high school, I realized that I could move people when I spoke. I realized that this carries with it a huge moral responsibility. When you have the ability to connect with people, you can do great harm as well as great good with it. And I always wanted to do good."

Govern Like a Girl

Canada has a big problem. We are a large, diverse country with lots of different people. Every person has their own unique set of opinions and knowledge and ideas and experiences. The people who govern our country—who get to make the rules—need to reflect this diversity of people in order to make decisions that help everyone.

Unfortunately, this is not the case today.

The vast majority of the people who have reached the top jobs in our governments are similar: older, white, straight men from fairly wealthy backgrounds. Almost 350 people have been in these top jobs and only 13 have been women so far! And Canada has never had a prime minister who is Black or racialized. Although all the territories have elected Indigenous premiers, no provinces have yet elected an Indigenous premier and only one has elected a racialized premier.

We need to see a greater diversity of people running in politics—and winning. The research is clear: achieving this will result in more perspectives being considered, better decisions being made, and greater equality in our country.

In other words, Canada needs *you*.

No one else has the exact same opinions and knowledge and ideas and experiences that you do. Other people may not be able to see the injustices that you can see or have the ideas that you do about how to fix them.

This book tells the stories of the women who have reached the top jobs in our governments. As girls, none of these women—none!—set out to be the premier or prime minister. Instead, these girls focused on solving the problems and injustices that they saw around them. Eva Aariak wanted her small community's Zamboni driver to clear the ice in Arctic Bay to give kids a place to play sports. Catherine Callbeck wanted to prove that girls could become successful businesspeople. Kathleen Wynne believed that girls should be allowed to wear pants to school if they want to. These girls pushed for the changes they wanted to see—*and when they did, change happened.*

These stories also show that there is no one background that someone needs to have to become one of our country's top leaders. These girls lived in every corner of our nation, from Burin, Newfoundland to Aklavik in the Northwest Territories to Surrey, British Columbia, and many places in between. Alison Redford had lived in more places around the world as a girl than some people will visit in a lifetime. Some of these girls grew up in comfortable households. Others did not. Caroline Cochrane experienced homelessness and lived on the streets of Yellowknife as a girl. Nellie Cournoyea was forced from her home and community to attend a residential school. Many of these girls also had very hard and sad things happen to them, like Kim Campbell's mother leaving her and moving overseas.

Questions for you:

- Have you ever experienced an **injustice**—a rule or decision or action that was unfair to a group of people, or that helped some people and hurt other people? What injustices have you seen other people experience?

- What would (and can) you do to address injustices in your school, or your community, or the world?

- Why do you think politics is important? Why does it matter who gets into politics?

As they grew up, all of these women were driven to make changes and solve problems in the world around them—and so they went into politics. Often, they ran against the odds. Both Christy Clark and Rachel

Notley helped their dads on campaigns as kids—even when their parties had little chance of success—and then went on to lead those same parties to historic victories. Women like Pauline Marois and Pat Duncan took big risks by running while pregnant, something that hadn't been done before. People told Kathleen Wynne that she couldn't win because she was a lesbian—and she ran and won, anyway.

For these women, it was not about the job; it was about the changes they wanted to see happen. They got the top jobs because they were willing to step forward and try to make change, even when it was hard or when the odds were stacked against them. They accomplished many amazing things that have helped people all across our country.

The word *govern* means making the rules. Governments make the rules, but every person in Canada has the opportunity to help shape those rules. All of the women in this book did exactly that. They didn't wait until they were in the top jobs to start pushing for changes; they pushed when they believed that changes were needed. And they started when they were girls.

Canada needs more of that. We need more girls pushing for change. We need more women—and a greater diversity of women—in government.

You don't need to change who you are, or what you look like, or where you're from, or what skills and talents and interests you have to become a leader. All you need is to find what you are passionate about and what changes you want to see in our country—and then *we* need *you* to act.

You can show up.

You can step up.

You can speak up.

You can govern like a girl.

Glossary of Terms

Cabinet: A group of people, almost always elected members from the governing political party, who make decisions about government policy. The members of the Cabinet are called cabinet ministers. Under the Westminster system of government in Canada, the prime minister (or premier) recommends to the governor general (or lieutenant governor) which people should be appointed to Cabinet.

Cabinet Minister: A member of Cabinet who is almost always responsible for a specific ministry. For example, the minister of finance is responsible for overseeing the government's money and budgets.

Candidate: At the federal and provincial levels, a person who is seeking elected office as a member of parliament (MP), a member of provincial parliament (MPP), or a member of the legislative assembly (MLA), for example. Sometimes this refers to a person seeking the leadership of a political party.

Coalition: A temporary coming-together of different political parties to hold the majority of seats in a legislature or parliament, allowing them to form a government.

Consensus Government: A system of government in which the group of people who have decision-making authority within government make decisions by seeking agreement from all people in the group rather than by a vote of majority.

Constituency: The group of people from a specific area who elect a politician (e.g., MP, MPP, MHA, MLA, or MNA) to represent them.

Constitution: The set of laws, rules, and conventions that set out the powers of government in a country. In Canada, that includes legislation such as the *Constitution Act, 1982*; the *Charter of Rights and Freedoms*; and the British North America Act, 1867. Some aspects of the Canadian constitution are unwritten conventions similar to those in other Westminster parliamentary systems, such as that of the United Kingdom.

Constitutional Amendment: A change to the Canadian constitution. To become law, most amendments need to be adopted by the House of Commons, the Senate, and at least two thirds of the provincial legislative assemblies that represent at least 50% of the Canadian population.

Council: At the municipal level, the group of elected officials in a municipality, which can be a village, town, or city. It is usually headed by a mayor, but in some places in Canada the head of the council is called a reeve, warden, or chair.

Election: An opportunity for all eligible voters to vote for the person they believe is best suited to represent them at a particular level of government. In a first-past-the-post election, whoever receives the most votes in a particular electoral district is elected to the position (MP, MPP, MHA, MLA, MNA, councillor, mayor, and so on).

First Minister: The prime minister (at the federal level) or the premier (at the provincial level), sometimes called *primus inter pares*, which is Latin for "first among equals." The first minister holds a special position in the Westminster parliamentary system of government, usually regarded as the most powerful position in the whole government. He or she is formally appointed by the governor general (or lieutenant governor). The first minister is, by convention, the leader of the political party that can command the confidence of the House of Commons (or legislative assembly).

First Nations: A term that refers to a broad range of Indigenous peoples whose ancestors lived in what is now called Canada more than 10,000 years ago. There are hundreds of First Nations in Canada with their own members and distinct and shared cultural practices, languages, and histories.

Glass Ceiling: A phrase used to describe an invisible barrier that prevents a group of people, such as women, from reaching higher places in an organization or system.

Government: A group of people, some elected (like MPs, MPPs, MHAs, MLAs, or MNAs) and some not elected (like deputy ministers, directors general, or program officers). The elected officials make decisions on how to raise funds from the public (usually through taxes) and how to spend those funds (on things like health care, national or provincial parks, and social supports) and pass laws. The elected officials who are part of Cabinet, known as cabinet ministers, are responsible for carrying out the government's agenda. The non-elected people, often known as civil servants, carry out the decisions made by Cabinet.

House: The place where the elected members gather to introduce, debate, and vote on legislation. The House of Commons (at the federal level) and the legislative assemblies (at the provincial level) are made up of elected members.

Incumbent: A person who currently occupies an elected position.

Inuit: A group of Indigenous people whose ancestors lived in the Northern region of what is now called Canada more than 10,000 years ago.

Leadership Race: An election within a political party to determine who will be the leader of the party. Usually, only members or supporters of the party may vote in the leadership race.

Majority Government: Government run by a political party that has a majority of the members of the House.

Mayor: The head of a council, usually elected directly by voters in the municipality.

Member of Parliament (MP): A person elected by the eligible voters in an electoral district to represent them in the federal House of Commons and to help constituents navigate government programs at the federal level, usually for a four-year term.

Member of Provincial Parliament (MPP): A person elected by the eligible voters in an electoral district to represent them in the legislative assembly of Ontario and to help constituents navigate government programs at the provincial level, usually for a four-year term.

Member of the House of Assembly (MHA): A person elected by the eligible voters in an electoral district to represent them in the legislative assembly of Newfoundland and Labrador and to help constituents navigate government programs at the provincial level, usually for a four-year term.

Member of the Legislative Assembly (MLA): A person elected by the eligible voters in an electoral district to represent them in the legislative assembly and to help constituents navigate government programs at the provincial level, usually for a four-year term.

Member of the National Assembly (MNA): A person elected by the eligible voters in an electoral district to represent them in the national assembly of Québec and to help constituents navigate government programs at the provincial level, usually for a four-year term.

Minority Government: A government run by a party that does not include a majority of the members of the House of Commons or provincial legislature. In this situation, the governing party must seek support from other parties in order to advance its policies and agenda.

Non-confidence: A vote that demonstrates that the members of the House of Commons or legislative assembly do not have confidence in the governing party. This is usually reserved for important matters, like the budget or key government priorities, which are treated as "confidence matters." Sometimes a vote of non-confidence is introduced as an explicit motion by an opposition party.

Non-partisan: Not belonging to any political party. Non-partisan politicians, as in the Northwest Territories, all run for office as independents.

Opposition: In the Westminster parliamentary system, the party that has the second-most seats in the House or legislative assembly forms the "official opposition." While the governing party is responsible for implementing its agenda, the opposition is responsible for holding the governing party to account by scrutinizing legislation and budgets.

Parliament: Sometimes used incorrectly to refer to the House of Commons. At the federal level it refers to both "chambers" of parliament—the House of Commons and the Senate. Because it includes these two chambers, the federal parliament in Canada is known as a bicameral system (Latin for "two rooms"). Provincial and territorial parliaments in Canada are unicameral—there is no Senate at the provincial level.

Plebiscite: A question put directly to eligible voters in a jurisdiction in order to determine what course of action should be taken. It is sometimes referred to as a referendum (plural: referenda) and is more common at the municipal level but rare at the provincial or federal levels.

Political Party: An organization, usually made up of members or supporters, who share common values and political objectives. Political parties nominate or put forward candidates in federal and provincial elections, one in each electoral district. In Canada, political parties must be registered at the federal or provincial levels, although some are allowed at the municipal level as well.

Politics: In Canada, a sphere of human activity that determines who is elected to make decisions on behalf of its citizens.

Premier: The first minister of a province or territory. In Québec, in French, the premier is called the *premier ministre*—the prime minister.

Prime Minister: The first minister of Canada.

Provinces: The country of Canada includes ten provinces, which are political units within the Canadian federation with their own legislative assemblies, elected members, and civil servants. The division of powers in the Canadian constitution sets out which level of government (federal or provincial) is responsible for which spheres of activity. For example, the provinces are responsible for education and health, and the federal government is responsible for national defence. In practice, there are many areas of shared responsibility.

Public Service: A broad term that refers to non-elected government employees. These employees, at the federal or provincial level, are sometimes referred to as "civil servants" and carry out the directions of Cabinet. They are non-partisan, so they take direction from whichever political party commands the confidence of the House.

Riding: An electoral district at the federal or provincial level. The number of people in each electoral district varies—there are generally more people in urban electoral districts and fewer in rural electoral districts. Each electoral district or riding elects one member at the federal and provincial levels.

Senate: The upper chamber of parliament, responsible for reviewing legislation passed by the House of Commons. Senators are appointed by the governor general on the advice of the prime minister. The process of choosing senators has varied over time. The constitution sets out how many senators may be appointed from each province, and senators, once appointed, may serve until they are 75 years old.

Territories: The country of Canada includes three territories, political units within the Canadian federation with their own legislative assemblies, elected members, and civil servants. The territories are Nunavut, Yukon, and the Northwest Territories.

Vote: In an election, the act of indicating which candidate should be chosen as the representative for an electoral district. Within a decision-making body, such as a federal or provincial legislative assembly or a municipal council, the act of indicating support or opposition to a motion or proposed legislation.

Acknowledgements

When I was a girl, I never imagined that politics was a place for someone like me. I thought that politicians were important people who were
far away, in every sense, from the small town where I lived.

Not enough girls in Canada aspire to be in politics. Not enough girls—
nor a diverse enough group of girls—grow up to govern. Part of the
reason is because Canadian girls have seen so few women in our most
senior political roles that they may not imagine themselves in those
positions someday.

As is often said, girls must see her to be her.

This is the motivation for this book. Although few in number, Canada has had some remarkable women in our most senior political roles. I had an opportunity to interview these women for Canada 2020's *No Second Chances*, a podcast about women in politics. I found the stories of Canada's female first ministers to be inspiring, motivating, and empowering. My hope is that Canadian girls will, too.

I owe great thanks to many people who contributed to this project. First and foremost, I want to thank the extraordinary women featured in this book. They represent an important part of Canada's history and have inspired more people than they know—including me. I also want to thank the *No Second Chances* team at Canada 2020 who enthusiastically supported this exploration, including Alex Paterson, Mira Ahmad, Sarah Turnbull, Aaron Reynolds, and Adam Caplan. This book benefitted from thoughtful feedback from Susan Graham, Lee Helmer, Pam Hrick, Jonathan Scott, Orla Rose Fleet, Greta Fleet, Emma Harmos, and Rachel Harmos. Sarah Kabani provided invaluable political research and editing assistance, supported by Huron University College and the McGorman Family Faculty Development Fund. I also want to thank Andrea Knight and Margie, Gillian, Jordan, Melissa, and the team at Second Story Press for believing in this project and working with me (through pregnancy and a pandemic!) to see it through to completion. Finally, I thank Jesse for being a true partner in every sense and baby Flora for being the inspiration for this book.

About the Author

Kate Graham researches, writes, speaks, and teaches about politics in Canada. She holds a PhD in Political Science from the University of Western Ontario and teaches in the Political Science Departments at Western and Huron University College. Kate is the creator and host of *No Second Chances* (NoSecondChances.ca), a Canada 2020 podcast about the rise and fall of women in Canada's most senior political roles—a project that inspired her own political pursuits and this book.

Kate lives with her partner, Jesse, and daughter, Flora, in London, Ontario.